Old Winter

Old Winter

Anne Le Dressay

Ottawa 2007

Old Winter
© 2007, Anne Le Dressay

Cover design by Tanya Sprowl
Layout by Jennifer Mulligan
Back cover author sketch by Heather Spears

Printed and bound in Canada
by Custom Printers, Renfrew, Ontario

Chaudiere Books
858 Somerset Street West
Main Floor
Ottawa, Ontario
K1R 6R7

www.chaudierebooks.com
email: info@chaudierebooks.com

Library and Archives Canada Cataloguing in Publication

Le Dressay, Anne M., 1949-
    Old winter / Anne Le Dressay.

Poems.
Includes index.
ISBN 978-0-9783428-0-7

    I. Title.

PS8573.E344O43 2007   C811'.54   C2007-906528-7

This book is dedicated to my mother
Margaret Le Dressay
and to the memory of my father
John Le Dressay (1913-1983)

Table of Contents

Small moments   9

Another story altogether

Attention   13
Skinning the weasel   14
That spring   15
Understanding nothing   16
Elaine, the hired girl   17
In the hallway by the stairs   18
I stepped out   19
Farm accident   21
I killed Santa Claus   22
The boy across the road   24
A man's job   25
Another story altogether   26
First blood   27
Spring: sixteen years old   28
Grey with an 'e'   29
Fences   31
Pan-American Games, Winnipeg, 1967   33
A small thing   35
Parlez-vous français?   37
The blind man   39
Country girls   41
Even the cockroaches   43
The house of wrong numbers   45

About that cobweb

Heading south   49
Racket   51
And the meek shall inherit   52
There is always dust   53
Nothing stays the same   55
The cemetery on the hill   56
Angels are everywhere   57
Being good   59
Circle   60
Paul Simon among the office towers   61
Browsing: another kind of travel   62
About that cobweb   64
In my cool cool basement apartment   66
Prozac poem   67

About that cobweb (cont'd)

    Good enough   69
    Anna in my dreams   71
    Bending   72
    Heirlooms   73
    Crone   75
    All my ghosts are useful   76
    Still in the world   77
    With new eyes   78
    Letter looking forward   79
    Even love   81

The real world

    Ice fog   85
    Every morning   86
    In the ravines   87
    Men in hard hats   88
    The man who plays musical instruments   89
    This scientist   90
    The real world   91
    Where the railyards were (Edmonton 1998)   92
    Cat Among the Boots   94
    Northern morning meditation   95
    Slow morning at the coffeeshop   96
    Icicles   97
    A skunk that dies on Saskatchewan Drive   99
    Millennial weather   100
    Late October, late afternoon in the office   101
    At the next table   102
    Coffee break   103
    But   104
    A ritual goodbye   105
    Neighbour   106
    Upon my skin   107
    End of the day in the student coffeehouse   108
    From my office window   109
    PD Day in the historic train station   110
    Renovation   111
    Pushing the wind   112
    Old winter   113

Small moments

Occasions silence me:
the turn of the midnight hour at the millenium,
the falling towers.

I am the laureate of small moments:
the shiny penny on the sidewalk,
the small talk in the café,
a red leaf or
the brief bond of a stranger's
smile.

Another story altogether

Attention

When I was born, their attention was
divided. Even my mother's (at least in part).
She wanted to be in the hospital, but she was
in the back seat of a car that crawled down snaking
roads in fog. I compelled her attention
by being born—
        there in the car.

My father's attention was on his driving, slow and
dangerous in the fog. He drove with the car door open,
leaning out to see the road, aware that if he miscalculated,
he could plunge us down a steep drop into the valley.
He didn't even stop the car
        when I was born.

My brother, just over a year old, had been dragged
out of sleep and taken out in the pre-dawn clammy cold,
bewildered. When I squalled, he paid attention.
I complicated his life just by showing up:
he would never again be
        the only one.

I forced them to pay attention. I came on the scene
with such drama that I used up my quota for
years to come. Since then, I have been ambivalent
about attention focussed on me. It attracts
and decentres. I prefer
        background, sidelines.

I carry subliminal memories of the world's
cold welcome in the
        clammy dark.

Skinning the weasel

I watched my father skin a dead weasel.
He slit it open down the belly and up the inside
of each leg. He pulled the fur off the limbs
and body as cleanly as if it were a coat.
The pink flesh gleamed and did not bleed.

He did this by the light of a trouble lamp
hung from the wall at the back of the old barn.
The wall was made of bales of straw,
piled on one another like bricks, and held
in a framework of untrimmed wooden poles.
In the lamplight, the walls shone golden.
Somewhere in the dark beneath the walls,
garter snakes curled and slept.

In the other stalls at the back of the old barn,
the two horses twitched their tails.
In the other part of the barn, cattle snuffled.
A cat or two curled up in hidden places in the straw.

It was dark, and I was still up, so it was winter.
The weasel's fur was white, so it was winter.
I watched as my father peeled the fur from
the gleaming flesh, undressing the weasel
as easily as he removed his own coat.

Except for the absence of buttons or zippers.
Except for the knife.

That spring

That spring morning, my father drove us to school
by horse and wagon. We crossed the frozen surface
of a creek that ran so small in summer we barely noticed it.
Now it was wide and white, and it cracked
beneath the weight of the wagon.

When we walked home later—Barry and my brother
and I—the ice was gone, and the creek ran wild
and turbulent. My father and Barry's father
waited for us, wearing hip-waders.
They carried us across on their backs.

I don't remember how high the water reached
on their legs. I remember how carefully
Barry's father walked as I clung to his back, how he felt
his way through the turbulence, testing the footing
with each step.

I could feel the tug of water against him, his resistance
a shudder through all his bones. In that shudder,
I felt the water telling me what it would do
if I tried to cross alone: how it would take me
in a hundred hands, toss me from one to another
like a twig; how it would pull me down and under,
slip its liquid fingers into my clothes, my boots,
my lungs; how it would claim me.

Understanding nothing

"Left   Left   Left Right Left"— the military beat
stomped out in perfect rhythm. And we march,
raising dust in the summer sun, a parade
without spectators, a parade fourteen strong
on the deserted roads around the school where
only the cows and the startled gophers see us.

This is field day practice for the marching competition.
We are arranged in stepladder fashion, the two tallest
at the front, carrying the school banner. I, six years old
and understanding nothing, am last in a trailing column.

And then the day itself, all the little one-room schools
represented, marching now in a real parade with real
spectators: people sparsely scattered along the two streets
of the one-elevator village. The military beat drummed
into me (by no real drum, only the teacher's voice),
I never miss a step. Nor ever will, for years to come,
whenever that beat finds me.

My body takes care of itself, and I, unaware
of being spectacle, watch the unimagined spectacle
of people standing in their yards and along the street,
watching. I am six years old, farm-grown, have
thirteen schoolmates. There is no name in my experience
for this experience.

It is a day of firsts. My school wins first prize
in the marching competition. I play my first game
of dodgeball, taste my first gum.
                    I go through the day
in a state of wonder, doing as I'm told and understanding
nothing: not dodgeball, not gum (which will not let me
swallow it), not the point
            of first prize.

Elaine, the hired girl

She was a neighbour's daughter.
She was hired to help out
the summer of my mother's sixth child
(the oldest not yet eight and summer
the busy season on the farm).
She washed clothes in the old wringer washer,
hung them on the line to dry,
gathered them later, folded them neatly.
She pulled weeds in the garden.
She fed the chickens.

I hovered under the flapping damp sheets on the line.
I hovered at the edge of the garden.
I hovered among the chickens.
I followed her from the house to the garden
to the chicken house, not speaking.
When she spoke to me, I did not answer,
only looked at her.

I was only six. She was thirteen.
It was to me as if a goddess
walked in my familiar space:
one did not speak, one gazed
with awe.

In the hallway by the stairs

Shadows in the hallway by the stairs
where the bookcase was that held the dictionaries,
the encyclopedia, and the collection of children's stories
in twelve volumes—*My Book House*—from
nursery rhymes in Volume One to stories
out of history in Volume Twelve.

Wash your hands first, my mother would say.
Those books were Sunday-special, Sunday-clean.

So there I was on the floor, cross-legged or
sitting on my heels or with my back against the wall,
reading.

I met Cinderella and Snow White and the twelve
dancing princesses. I met Babba Yagga and
Peer Gynt and Ariel, Daniel Boone and
George Washington.

The shadows in the hallway dissolved.
The narrowness of my everyday life fell away.
I forgot how small my world was, how small I was.
I forgot that I *was* at all.

My body cramped in a dark corner,
my mind moved in worlds without boundary,
luminous with possibility.

I stepped out

I stepped out from the back of the wine-dark
'54 chevy. I stepped out onto gravel that rolled
treacherous underfoot, unfamiliar. I was used to shale,
also treacherous, but which
                              slid.

On the back seat, books slid over each other
like shale. The schoolyard was vast and alien:
concrete sidewalk, swings, see-saw, bicycle stand,
too many running, screaming kids,
and no trees.

Erase. Roll back the thunder and hail
that brought me to this gravelled October schoolyard.
Roll back the wind that caved in the roof of the old barn,
blew a granary across the yard, chickens to their death,
two windows in and hail into my brothers' beds,
blew us off the farm
                       for good.

Erase. Return to the grassy schoolyard
with its dim stable and its border of trees
which were swing, see-saw, and jungle gym
in one.
                              Return
to the one room with its 14 students and its
one-shelf library at the back and the teacher
            who let me spend half the day at the library shelf.

There. Continue there, and I grow up
not a stranger, not an outsider, not a foreigner,
not an alien. I grow up with those who are
not enemies.

Instead, the October morning
and the sun shining on the new school, on concrete,
on too many children, on unfamiliar gravel
that rolled underfoot,
                      treacherous.

Farm accident

She died, he sprained his wrist,
and I saw my first dead person—

she in a white coffin in their living room,
4 years old forever, her hair in golden
curls, her face waxy white, like
the hard plastic of a doll's face, or
the storybook drawing of a princess.

Not real.

"Isn't she beautiful?" the older sister said,
standing beside me as I stared and
stared. The sister was 10. I was 7.
I did not know what to say to a *big kid*
who in ordinary life ignored me, and
whose little sister had become
cold plastic. I wanted to giggle and
not be there.

The gap was too great between the stiff
white doll-in-a-box and us who stood around
in our ordinary selves. It was impossible
to believe she had ever raced around
the farmyard, climbed haystacks, scrambled
onto the tractor for a ride with her brother,

who, 8 years old (in the background now
and choosing background for all the years
I knew him) had overturned the tractor

and sprained his wrist.

I killed Santa Claus

Seven years old and in a new school,
I told the girl next door
that Santa Claus didn't exist.
She resisted, but was defeated
by my utter disbelief—the blank
cynicism of the lifelong atheist
meeting her first true believer.

I had barely even heard
of Santa Claus when I killed him.

At the other school, there was an oddity
in red suit and fake white beard,
who called our names at the family
Christmas party, and we had to go to the front
and get a present. But he didn't matter.

What mattered was that the present was
from Arnold, who (I had decided,
not consulting him) was my boyfriend.
Arnold had drawn my name. So what
if it was chance? It was Arnold,
and I thrilled at my first experience
of the meant-to-be.

Santa Claus was a minor figure in the drama,
and a year later at another school
I killed him with my disbelief that anyone
believed. To me it was like thinking
you could meet angels or Snow White.

I stood out on the December gravel road
between her house and mine,
and the girl next door gave me Santa Claus
in the taken-for-granted way of total faith.
Just handed him over. And I
killed him.

The boy across the road

The boy across the road liked me.
His father owned the store
where we bought milk and the Sunday
ice-cream treats and sometimes
chocolate bars or candy or gum
with our weekly allowances.

The boy across the road had candy at will,
comics. He gave me gum, blackballs.
Once he tried to give me licorice ropes,
black, but I didn't believe they were candy.
They looked too much like something
my brother might try to fool me with,
and the boy across the road was,
after all, a boy.

I didn't know what it meant that he
liked me, except presents.
He did things for me he wouldn't
for my brother. So, instructed by
my brother, I asked to borrow comics,
pretending tastes not my own.

The boy across the road liked me a lot.
I didn't know then what that meant, but
my brother did, and it was my brother

I wanted to please.

A man's job

When my father worked shifts,
he was the one who dealt with daytime
neighbourhood crises that called for a man.

He was the only man around the day a local dog
crossed the line from temperamental to dangerous—
the dog that had once turned on me for no reason,
growling and lunging. Then for no reason
turned away. That dog.

The day they called my father,
the dog attacked a pig. Two women
put themselves between the dog and the pig,
and though the dog did not attack the women,
it would not give up trying to get past them
to the pig.

I remember people talking about
their bravery and quick thinking. But
this situation called for a man.

Somebody ran for my father. Somebody ran
for her husband's rifle. My father shot the dog.
He didn't shoot the pig, though it had to be killed
later, its snout too badly torn.

He shot the dog. Matter-of-fact,
the only man around, accepting
a man's job.

Another story altogether

Not my story, but the other one
that was there all along, tangled with mine
and utterly separate, breathing at night
in the bed across the room, while I lived
my own story. My own. Small, centred,
mine, that talked my words and saw
through my eyes.

This other story sees it through her eyes,
and they are 3 years younger and a different
colour. It's not the same family and not the same
traumas. The family is 3 years older when she
starts remembering, and there are more people in it.

Two stories, two worlds barely touching,
the light hitting the same things at such
different angles they are not the same things
at all. To her, I am part of the world outside of
her, in which she must find or make a place.
To me, *she* is outside.

You'd think it would be the same house at least,
the same bedroom. But she was afraid of the dark
and I wasn't. We had a fair and equal arrangement:
one night, the door closed tightly for me, the next
night, left open a crack for her.

Only now does it occur to me to wonder
if, every second night when the door was closed
to spare me the small distraction of that
shaft of light, she lay awake, facing alone
the terrors of the dark,
while I slept.

First blood

An outhouse at the edge of a wood
beside a river that in dry summers
shrank to green stinking mud. An outhouse
on the border between wood and garden.

Dark blood staining my underwear.

Thirteen years old. Babysitting at a neighbour's.
Transition summer between the two-room
country school and the composite high school
in the village.

Alone. Nobody to tell and no desire to tell.
Just another secret to absorb into the tangle
of secrets I held close, as if secrets meant
safety.

Late June. An outhouse with a grey
wooden seat. Flies. That smell of maturing
shit, cut by whispers of fresh air from the mesh
of screen over the small high window.

Overhanging branches sheltering the roof.
Sunshine and shadows. Wood and garden.
Freshness and rot. The hard-packed earth
of the path to the house.

First blood and a matter-of-fact thought:
Well, there it is.

Spring: sixteen years old

In March, a blizzard closed the school for three days
and piled snow to the eaves—a storm for legend.

In April followed a flood for legend.
There never was another spring with so much water spread
so far and catching so much silver from the sun.
The snow was dead. It lay in shrunken dirtstreaked
dunes and the flooded fields swallowed its raw edges,
sunlight laughing from the waves and dancing
swift hypnotic beauty to the eyes—
sparkling, dazzling, blinding.

That was when he came, a new boy in school,
a refugee from high water.
He came when the snow sank into quiet oblivion
in fields that were bluer than blue.
He was the colour of that spring, his eyes the blue
of field and sky, his hair the gold of sunlight.

And when I think of him, I think of endless water
catching at my eyes in silver dancing joy;
and I think of his eyes reaching for the horizon
across unclouded distance; and I think of sunlight
catching in his golden hair and tossing light,
so that he dazzled
like the watery world in sunlight.

He came when winter melted into water and light.
He left when the river drew its riches to itself and bared
the sodden fields to drying winds,

and the world was once again
ordinary.

Grey with an 'e'

You live in a seedy hotel and share a bathroom
with 6 others. When the city was Vancouver,
the hotel was on Powell, which somebody told me
had the roughest bars in town, where nobody went
who didn't carry steel. (I can't imagine you
carrying steel.)

You leave town—whatever town—on impulse,
dumping everything you own (books, clothes,
furniture). Your car breaks down and
you walk away, thumb out as if you'd never
forked over cash, signed papers. You promise
letters you never write. You voice plans you
never pursue. You deliver flyers and call Mom
collect 6 times a year and nobody else ever.
When she dies, you will disappear.

When you were 8 and I was 18, one autumn evening
we ran. Just to run. Just because. We ran
through the tall grass in the ditches, the grass
that pulled at our legs and made the run a struggle.
We ran shrieking because the air was raw with
evening and with the cool dank smell of fall and
because something in the coming night was wild.
We ran till we were breathless, and then fell flat
on our backs on the earth, and our bodies cooled
as the dark deepened. We watched the stars come out,
you and me, breathing deep of the earth smell and
the cool intoxication of the sky.

Now we live at opposite ends of the country.
I live in a condo with a mortgage I would sometimes
like to walk away from the way you walk away
from your dead cars. I have too many years
of education and a job they call professional.
When I move, my friends groan at the boxes of books.
I write letters home, visit every year or two, get
your news from Mom.

We were in the same city for a year once.
You stayed with me and then I stayed with you
and then I haven't seen you since.
I drop the occasional letter into the blankness
that never responds. I drop the letter because
you still call Mom.

There was a guitar.
There was *Drawing on the Right Side of the Brain*.
There was a single letter you wrote to me
that was so clear that reading it was like
drinking fresh water.
There was a startled moment when a connotation
connected us (*Grey* with an *e* is not the same
colour as *gray* with an *a*. Nobody else knew
what I meant.)

I cannot put these together with
the seedy hotels.

When I was 23 and you were 13,
people sometimes mistook us for each other.
Even Mom did a double-take once or twice.
I sometimes think you are my twin.
I sometimes ache not to go home again.
I will not try to stop you when you disappear.

Fences

They did not believe in fences, but in the innate
nobility and right to freedom of all living things.

We might wake to the gobbling of a flock of turkeys
filling the front yard, or meet the bull out strolling
as we walked home. Us locals, hardened to fences
and the need to curb invasions, we thought them
naïve, irresponsible, or silly. They didn't fit.

Nor did their horse—a slender grey creature
who chased the paper boy up their front steps,
where the boy ran into the house without knocking,
the horse clattering onto the front porch after him.
Playful, the owners said. The paper boy
refused to deliver anyway.

The horse was not the kind we were used to seeing—
not the slow, dull, brown horse that pulled a wagon
or a sled on the occasional farm. The grey horse
was a frivolity. He grazed or galloped in an unfenced
field or in a pasture with an open gate. He neighed
like a movie horse. He didn't work, though
         occasionally he carried a rider.

As he did in the Centennial Day parade, where he was
the only one to know what a parade should be.
His owner on his back, he moved proud, his neck arched,
his high-stepping walk a dance among the lumbering
tractors and home-made floats. He pranced, oblivious
to the absence of anything around him to match
his grace and beauty.

          Out of place as always, he dimmed
the already dim surroundings. He brought us ceremony,
showed us that ceremony could turn the ordinary
                                            magical,
and that the magical could touch
                                    us too.

Pan-American Games, Winnipeg, 1967

I remember no rain, no cloud that summer,
just bright skies and colour and music.
I was 17, bussing in from the country
every weekday to finish grade 12 biology
at the University of Winnipeg summer school.

Everything that summer was exotic to the eyes
of my country innocence, even the instructor,
his lab coat crisply white against the dark richness
of his skin. Even he was Pan-American.

I remember colour, streets crowded with athletes
and visitors, a calypso band that played
at Eaton's every afternoon.

I bought no tickets to anything official.
I found my entertainment in the streets and
the downtown public places: in the faces,
in the sheer numbers of people on the sidewalks,
in the out-of-province, the out-of-country
license plates—as if a continent had come to me
from every province and state and even further.

I kept an eye on license plates, filling in the map
of the continent in my head. The crowning piece
came from Central America. I did not need
the license plate to know it was the prize—

the vehicle a travel- and time-worn station wagon
crawling down a busy street beside The Bay, its
occupants hanging out its windows with amazement
in their faces. They had come a long way.
They had come to a place they had only partially
believed in when they set out. Their faces said so,
with smiles and wonder.

I too, seeing them, had come to a place I had not
imagined and to a city I had not known this plain
prairie city could ever be in any summer, even
that summer of endless sun.

A small thing

A small thing happened on this dirt road
from nowhere to nowhere, a back road between
fields where no houses were.

A summer shower turned the dirt to mud and
clogged the wheels of a bicycle.
There was no traffic at all, no traffic in sight
except distantly on the highway.
Just the mud and the cyclist miles from home
with a bike she could not abandon
because it was not hers.

The wooden bridge within sight, the bridge with
no side rails, so narrow only one car could cross
at a time. Nothing happened. But what *could?*

> *The one car on a muddy road*
> *not a friendly neighbour. The one car*
> *driven by a bad guy who wants to get you*
> *under the bridge, and what do you do?*
> *Only the fields and no houses.*
> *Only the bush and the deep ditch and*
> *the long grass and the mud.*
> *Only the lonely spot on a lonely day*
> *and you can't get home.*

Nothing happened. The one car on the muddy road
was a friendly neighbour, a real one. He put the bike
in the trunk and drove her to the highway (the long way
home), then cleared the mud from the wheels before
leaving her to the rest of her adventure: a flat tire,
another summer shower, a friendly stranger driving her
to the gas station so she could call home, then her father
annoyed and refusing to drive out to pick her up 3 miles
from home with her brother's useless bike, so
she would have walked, pushing it all the way,
but her brother came.

Parlez-vous français?

A knock at the door of my furnished room
in a downtown Winnipeg rooming house
where I study in the afternoons.
I open to the woman from the next room,
and three weary-looking men.

They don't speak English. She knows
I speak French, though she does not know
how awkwardly.

I turn to the men: *Parlez-vous français?*

For seconds, they stand blank. Then one face
lights up, one spine straightens. He has been
butting against incomprehension all day for
how many days. He no longer expects
anything else and so is slow to realize
that he knows what I'm saying.

Oui! Such relief! I have never seen
such relief. He tells me they are looking
for rooms to rent. I translate for my neighbour,
he for his companions. I struggle against
the limitations of my French. I tell them
about the small apartment that takes up
the third floor, about a single room
downstairs. I go with them to look in case
they have questions.

It is the winter of 1968-69. They are Czech
refugees. I am a student. French is my
mother tongue, but I am not easy with it.
It is the first time my knowledge of it has done
anybody else any good:
       how his face shed its look
of blank discouragement, how his body shed
its weariness

when I spoke.

The blind man

Hit me, hit me, said the blind man
sitting beside me on the bus.
At his feet, his dog lay, making himself
as small as a large German shepherd can be.

Across from us, a woman had just told her child—
in a voice undecided between discretion
and self-display—that the dog would attack anyone
who threatened the blind man.

Hit me, hit me, he said to me, and I almost did,
knowing that the dog would maybe raise his head
but maybe not even that.

The dog liked me. When I dropped in once
to visit the blind man at work, the dog leaped up
so eagerly from his place under the desk
that he banged his head hard
on the edge of the desk.

Don't break my dog, the blind man said.

Before I met him, I used to see the blind man
at the university where we were both students.
He did not have the dog then. He carried a white cane.
I helped him across the street once, his hand
light on my arm, his shirt the green of new grass.

I met him when my roommate answered an ad
and began to read for him. When I had known him
a few weeks, he said he knew I was over 25 because
I did not try to impress him. He knew how tall I was
by where my voice came from when we walked together.

People thought he was psychic, he said, because
of how much he could tell from their voices and
the small sounds of their movements and gestures.
I thought about it and decided I didn't mind
what he knew about me that I hadn't told him.

We went out once or twice. We went to a bar.
We went to the *Festival du voyageur*,
riding the bus with his dog.
Hit me, he said, laughing under his breath,
his dog at his feet.

Country girls

Country girls,

he tells me, are sexier than city girls.
It is the early 70's. The sexual revolution
has begun, but a man can't yet count on it.

He means that country girls know more about sex
and are freer about it.

Country girls know more, he says,
because of the animal sex around them.
Dogs copulate in the schoolyard, cows
give birth in field or barn, bulls carry
their impressive penises in full sight.

He assumes not only that all this animal sex
is instructive to country girls, but also that
it turns them on.

He speaks out of stereotype and
hope,
once he knows I'm a country girl.

Not all country girls live on farms.
Not all farm girls are permitted the sight of animal sex,
or the knowledge that a bull's penis has any purpose
beyond telling a bull from a cow, or what it is
dogs are doing in the schoolyard that makes
some of the kids giggle.

Not all country girls have seen kittens
slip from under a cat's tail or a calf from a cow.
Nor does it follow that where there is knowledge,
there is also desire.

I keep these reflections to myself.
I know the stereotype is just that, but
I let him keep
his hope.

Even the cockroaches

When I came looking for an apartment,
he didn't ask for references. He asked me
where I worked. When I said, *The university*,
he was impressed. I knew he wanted to ask more,
but he didn't. I didn't tell him that my paid work
took 12 hours a week, that I was really a student,
that my savings were nearing oblivion.
He rented me the apartment. By then I knew
he just couldn't say no.

He couldn't say no to anyone else either.
The smell of marijuana sweetened the halls.
The previous tenants in my apartment had left
in a hurry, the caretaker said. They were wanted
for possession of stolen goods. They had not left
a forwarding address or informed their business
associates. For months, strangers buzzed me
from downstairs or knocked on my door,
asking for Kevin, whose name was carved
on one of the windowsills.

Turnover was high. The fugitive and the transient,
the slightly illegal and the eternally restless
found temporary shelter.

I was on the edge of dramas, in the margins of stories
more vividly coloured, more luridly violent than
my own. I felt like an extra in a movie whose script
I had not read. I was an outsider by the quietness
of my life.

I exchanged greetings with the young cop across the hall.
The landlord could not say no to the law any more
than he could to the lawless. Once or twice
I looked after the caretaker's small daughter
when he had errands to run (his wife was in the hospital).
Next door to the cop, a very large man would leave
his door open and listen for me and come out in the hall
to stare at me as I fumbled my keys. He would ask
innocuous odd questions that startled me
out of reserve and then
                                deeper in.

It was a world in which outward lives mixed easily:
favours asked and given, beds briefly shared. Reserve
was of a different kind than in my world.

Even the cockroaches living their secret lives in the walls
were more at home than I was.

The house of wrong numbers

I could have been a full service town:
hotel, drugstore, city and county offices,
provincial police *and* RCMP. Even 911.

Small-town-friendly callers expected me
to provide the number if mine wasn't the place
they wanted. Some would not believe.

The Johnson Motel no longer exists, I would say,
thinking about where it used to be—the building
transformed into student apartments with a reputation
for parties. And I would think, *You don't want
to stay there anyway.*

Some would ask for other hotels.
Some would ask where it had moved. One said,
But I got the number off the internet,
as if that guaranteed truth.

I got tired of wrong numbers interrupting
breakfast or a shower or the crucial moment
in a white sauce or a dream. I stopped answering
the phone and let the machine intervene:

>   *This is not the Johnson Motel.*
>   *This is not the drugstore.*
>   *This is not the police station.*
>   *If you know who you are calling,*
>   *leave a message.*

Some one told me, in deeply offended tones,
that I was rude. Wrong numbers are not?
Eventually I conceded this much
to small town expectations:

> *If you want the Johnson Motel, try the Twilight Zone.*
> *If you want the drugstore or the police station or any other*
> *business in town, try the phone book.*
> *You have reached 672-4441 (six sept deux,*
> *quarante-quatre, quarante et un).*
> *Leave a message.*

About that cobweb

Heading south

The blackest hour of a night without
moon or stars. The middle time without
residue of the day gone or hint of the one
to come. That hour the clock forgets
because nobody is awake to read it.

In that hour, I am awake and out
on the Calgary Trail somewhere between cities,
held in the circle of light from a single
streetlight, and I am talking to the police.
Two of them, one of me, a stopped car,
a single light, and the deep black.

They want to know who I am.
I have left my purse in my apartment in Edmonton
and my ID in my purse. I give them
the phone number, tell them my roommate
will vouch for me.

He is a night owl. He can stay up half the night,
mesmerized by the blue glow of the computer
screen, or drawn into the timeless pages of
a book. But this night, the phone pulls him
out of deepest sleep. It is the hour when
even he sleeps past his demons.

He tells them I am home,
goes to my room to make sure, tells them
I am in my bed, asleep.
The police tell me this, and I am held
in a wordless timeless moment, seeing
the shape of a sleeping body under
the covers on my bed.

Who took my place? Who took advantage
of my forgetfulness and attached herself
to my official ID in my legal home?
She sleeps my sleep, oblivious to the passing of
the blackest hour, and I stand in the glare
of a single streetlight, cut loose

in isolated darkness, heading south.

Racket

> *racket—confused clattering noise; clamor; commotion; clangor, clash, clatter, din, disturbance, fracas, jangle, riot, roar, ruckus, tumult, turmoil, uproar, wrangle.*

Noise without rhythm, noise without pulse.
Noise in which the ear can find no music, no beat
of heart or breath.

Racket makes my nerves stand up, my muscles tense.
It makes my bones shudder, my teeth clench,
my breath catch and hold, enduring.

Now I *am* the racket as I walk down the street
with my rattly metal shopping cart, clenched against
the clatter of my own progress.

I have thought out my route with care, planning for
the better sidewalks, the curbs that slope for wheelchairs
and strollers.

I had hoped the weight of my purchases would calm
the clatter, but metallic looseness outweighs
mere pounds.

Nobody else's shopping cart makes such a racket.

The bones of my hands are shivered from the jolting,
every bump travelling up the metal frame
to set the bones aquiver all the way up the spine.

I am a cloud of clangour, a confusion,
an uproar, a din. I am a commotion, a fracas,
a jangle, a riot, a ruckus, a tumult, a wrangle.

I am a walking noise.

And the meek shall inherit

Not this. Perhaps some post-
millenial earth where
lying low pays off in survival while
the loud and pushy get
clobbered.

Those who inherit this earth
are those who shout loudest, or who
simply take because they know
it's theirs.

If the meek inherit,
it's not anything as spacious or solid
or fecund as the earth.

Unless they taste it
in the dust kicked up
by the exuberant wheels of the true
inheritors taking off with their
inheritance.

There is always dust

Every time I move, I believe
(in some dim and inarticulate recess
of my brain) that in this new home, *this* one,
finally, there will be no dust.

The light will always be pure.
Everything I own will find its proper place
and settle there, glowing, and will continue to glow.

And I will too. I will be my best self
every day. I will no longer procrastinate. I will
sit at my desk, and the sun will fall upon my shoulders,
upon my head, upon my words, and I will write
clean and perfect poems.

But there is always dust.

There is the dust of former tenants
lodged in corners, at the backs of shelves, in
light fixtures and in walls. There is the dust I bring with me
in my cardboard boxes, in my furniture, in my
books. There is the dust of the house itself, and there is
the inescapable dust of myself, into which I fall
daily.

I sit down to write, and the sun is not a single
golden beam, but a glare that picks out every
speck and mote upon the floor, the shelves,
and in the mocking air itself. There is no
stillness. Phantom brooms and mops invade
the flow of words, chase away metaphors.

And I am still myself. I sit restless at my desk,
distracted by anxieties, nagged by the small guilt
stirred up by the phantom brooms. I still
wrestle with rags and pieces of words
that will not form one perfect shining shape.
Nothing changes. I am still myself and
there is always dust.

Nothing stays the same

Even when everything stays the same,
it does not. The light comes in
at a different angle every day until you get up
in daylight instead of darkness (or the reverse).
Underground, the seed stirs and wakes,
pushes thin shoots into the light,
and the world is green.

Even when nothing is happening, nothing
stays the same. The tree outside the window
grows. The brick of the wall drops a crumb
of stone. In the silent corners behind the furniture
where I never look, dust thickens and a spider
complicates its web. The death curled in
one or another of my cells has one less breath
of sleep.

In a room where nothing is happening,
a shaft of sunlight falls, and the dust motes
drift and dance.

The cemetery on the hill

This town looks towards death.
You come here when your real life is over,
when the farm has passed on to the next
generation or to strangers, or when
the smaller town can offer nothing
for your failing limbs and faltering hearts.
You focus now on doctors, hospitals, home care.
You come here to wait for death.

Even if you are here for other reasons,
you catch like a disease the poison in the air.
First, the sharpness and brightness dim.
You begin to think that the best that is left
in the world is *pretty* and *pleasant*.
You begin to think that *beautiful*, that *passionate*,
that *delightful* or *vibrant* or *intense* are exaggerations,
or that they are so long past that they rest
in the cemetery that looks down from a hill
upon the pleasant meandering ravine trails.

You see the placid lake and the well-groomed parks
as the epitome of the possible. You forget
mountain, ocean, storm. You forget
awe, rage, joy.

Angels are everywhere

Angels are everywhere these days—
book covers, calendars, jewelry
(your own guardian angel
glittering on a pin—
wear it on your lapel, or,
if you're shy about angels,
wear it on your bra strap).

Angels have caught on.
The curly-haired and pudgy-cheeked,
the infant angels have enraptured us
with their bland smiles and
cuteness.

Not for us those other Angels
we cannot control:
the one that wrestled Jacob
all the night into a new name,
the one that astounded Mary
with the mystery of God
within her.

Not for us the alien strangeness
that lays a burning coal
to a prophet's lips, that carries
Otherness in every step.

We have tamed the angels
and they are not tame.

Behind their painted cherub smiles,
they bide their time.
They hoard the light that lives
inside their eyelids.
They mouth their secret words.
When they are ready,
they will raise their eyes,
they will loosen their tongues,
and we will not be able to stand
before their blinding innocence.

We have tamed the angels
and they are not tame.

Being good

Being good is easy. All the *DON'T*'s
spelled out in the rule book:
*Don't steal. Don't kill. Don't
speak ill of the dead. Don't brag.
Don't break promises. Don't.*

The boundaries are clear.
Whether the rules are God's
or your mother's, you know
when you have broken them.

When you venture beyond
the rulebook, life is more vivid,
less sure: *Love God
with all your heart. Blessed
are the peacemakers. Be
kind.*

In that place, trails are unmarked.
Those who have gone before have left
only riddles: *Be willing to be blind.—
To reach satisfaction in all, desire its
possession in nothing.—All shall be well
and all shall be well.*

If you follow them towards the light,
you step first into darkness.
You make your way by guess, by hope,
by trust.

Circle

The hand holding my left hand
is cool, and the hand holding my right hand
is warm, and we stand in a circle
shaped like a pear or an almost-
figure-eight that no compass could trace.

We are limited by the size and shape
of the chapel. We are too many to make a circle
just here, but a circle is perfection, and the joined
hands symbolize unity, and so we hold hands
as we pray, each a link in a chain
for the moment unbroken.

Each link has oddnesses and hidden flaws.
Most of us know each other only superficially.
When we leave here, we become again
isolated units.

Briefly, our joined hands make us
each an equal part of something bigger.
One voice speaks, and the *Amen* we say
makes us one will. Briefly, we are
what we aspire to be—one voice
with one purpose, a circle.

Paul Simon among the office towers

Saturday afternoon.
The downtown coffeeshop
is almost empty, the office towers
silent, the coffeeshop free of its
weekday busyness.

The one staff person is distantly polite,
but he meets my eyes. He is real.

At one table, someone reads a newspaper.
At another, two people plan
a hostel-and-backpack trip across Europe.

I am the only other. I sit at the window,
watching sparse traffic, listening
to Paul Simon sing about the train in the distance.

It is March, winter edging into spring.
The city is grey concrete in sunlight.

I do not hear the train in the distance, but I do
think it's true. I hear its promise in the gaps of sky
between the stone towers, where Simon's voice
is a thread of wind.

Browsing: another kind of travel

Sometimes when I travel, I sleep in rooms
lined with books: study as guest room.
Friends pull out the hide-a-bed or put a mattress
on the floor and leave me their books
for company.
              And I travel again
as my eyes flick over book titles, catch and stop
where in another context they would
                                  glance past.

Animal Liberation. I read about chickens
turned into egg-laying machines, their feet
grown into the wire mesh of their cages;
about veal calves malnourished to keep their flesh
pale, confined in narrow stalls to prevent them
from licking up their own urine for salt.

Veal drops out of my diet. Eggs become a problem.

Freaks. I look at photos of people with extra limbs;
I read about the variations on Siamese twins, about
androgynes and bearded women. I recall anecdotes
from people who work in places where we hide our
freaks, more numerous than we admit.

'Normalcy' becomes an elastic word, stretching
easily to include my own (mild and invisible)
freakiness, turn it into mere eccentricity. Impassioned
discussions that condemn homosexuality or blame
the socially dependent are suddenly naïve and simplistic.

Death. A coffee table book by the looks of it.
But the color photos are of bodies at the morgue,
accident scenes, murder scenes. (Sixteen stab wounds,
this one, count the holes in the chest.)
                                      And how death comes
to creatures in the wild. By violence. Always.
(Hyenas eating alive a deer that cannot run
because it is giving birth.)

The world acquires new dimensions
                                of darkness.

In other people's studies, when I travel,
I travel again.
                    And my mind changes.
I can feel the shifting, the world adjusting
                                      as I read.

About that cobweb

He asks if I am a perfectionist, and I have
no answer. About some things I am
meticulous, but.

"For instance," he says, "do you care
about that cobweb hanging from the ceiling
over there?" He gestures towards
my dining room.

No, I don't care about the cobweb.
I can't even see it. A day later
I'm still looking for the cobweb, which he
perhaps invented. I don't care
about the cobweb or the dust or the clutter
of books and the mess of papers.

Clutter is poetic. Mess is full of surprises.
Out of chaos came
                    all particular things—
the wood in the walls and ceilings and in the
frame of the bed, and also the dustballs
under the bed and the cobwebs
hanging from the ceiling.

                 In the meditative stillness
under the bed, various minute particles (dust,
cat hair, my hair, the invisible emanations of my
living and aging) find each other and build
intricate frail structures that have
                      their own perfection.

Clutter reflects the world inside that is
not, is never,
                clean lines and polish, never
orderly—the stirring, thriving, fertile inner world
out of which
                come dreams, come
visions, come intimations and intuitions, *Eureka* and
the angels
        he claims to believe in.

In the tangled soft cavern that is my unmade bed,
the Muse lingers.

In my cool cool basement apartment

Spiders have had babies in my cool cool
basement apartment with its floor of golden
stone so cool and smooth underfoot
and its deep marble windowsills.

Spiders have been fruitful and their progeny
have no enemy but their own numbers.

From ceiling to baseboard, webs and
single threads become dustily visible
in every angle and corner.

Everything that does not move
is connected to something else—
the clock to the headboard it sits on,
the toaster to the counter, the cat's dish
to the floor, one lamp to another.
Invisible threads slide sticky fingers
across my skin as I walk through my rooms.

Little spiders, barely visible, hang from
cupboard doors, from utensils I take from a
drawer, from the top rim of my glasses.
They scuttle for safety as I pick up the dishcloth,
or a book I was reading this morning.

I battle the invasion with broom and vacuum cleaner,
but the fine sticky threads reappear.
I begin to fear that one morning I will wake
like Gulliver, staked to the bed by multitudinous
silken cords while busy weavers bind me
tighter, closer, connecting me finally, visibly,
irrevocably to everything I own.

Prozac poem

I am not myself. I am
at the mercy of moods—sudden
plunges into moroseness, leaps
into rage, shifts into sensitivity
so raw it is as if I had no skin.

Prozac, says the doctor. Now

nothing touches me. At work,
where there is more work than time,
and where management turns over so
quickly that nobody in charge knows
what should be happening, co-workers
gossip and complain, grow short-
tempered, take stress leave. I

stay even, not rocked by the rocking
boat, *happy*. I am caught up in
hilarity. I joke. I laugh. I talk too loud.
I wear a constant uncharacteristic
grin. I become what, even on prozac,
I consider obnoxious.

I am not myself, but I am fascinated
by this not-self: extroverted, bold, upbeat,
unflappable.

I am on holiday from the stress
of being me. Not only from the mood
swings, but also from a characteristic
caution, an undercurrent of melancholy,
and even the ability to feel another's pain.

It is a relief, in spite of holes in my
memory, various physical upsets, and
the constant awareness that my emotions
are out of sync with the world.

For a time, it is restful, but holiday turns
into banishment, and the division between
self and self deepens into wound. I

quit prozac. Post-holiday—the mood swings
somewhat tamed, and none of the rest of
me absent—I am glad to be home again,
to take up the mundane and familiar,
to find myself again

myself.

Good enough

He tells me that
if I join an internet chat group,
I can be whoever I want.

I can be a 21-year-old
super-model.

Perhaps he thinks this to be
the secret fantasy
of every middle-aged woman.

He is too young to drink or vote.
He lives on line, chatting
electronically
with people halfway around the world
or just across the room.
He lives several lives
at once.

To his mind, he is
opening my eyes to exciting
possibilities.

He doesn't know that,
even at 21, I didn't want to be 21.
I wanted to be older.

Or that what I crave is not
the limelight, but
anonymity.

Or that I have never wanted to be
a model of any kind or super
of any kind.

Good enough
is good enough for me.

Anna in my dreams

In my fantasies, I am almost myself.
I take one step to the side.
I change the final vowel of my name
to give it extra weight, an extra moment in the world.

In my dreams, I am *Anna*, not *Anne*.
Not so plain. More solid. The same, coming and going.
That solid. That balanced. In my dreams, *Anna*
has more presence, more staying power
than *Anne* ever could. *Anne* is barely a breath.

Annie doesn't do it, has never done it.
Annie is a diminishment, a falling away.
Annie is less.

I have tried out *Anne-Marie*, but I am
not that complicated, and *Marie* is a foreigner,
even though the name is everywhere in my family.

If you call me *Annie*, I will ask you not to.
If you call me *Anne-Marie*, I will answer
with only a moment's pause.
If you call me *Anna*, I will answer without pause,
and I will not correct you, though I am Anna

only in my dreams.

Bending

I still thrill at finding
a shiny dime on the sidewalk.
I still bend for it. I even bend for
pennies, though I've known
for a long time their cash value is
cancelled out by the time and energy
expended in bending

It's not cash value I care about.
It's the fact of finding—a vestige
from childhood when pennies added up
to a chocolate bar, a bottle of pop.
I would scour the ditches for empties:
one cent for beer bottles, two cents for pop.
A shiny dime then meant a treat, something
extra. There was still penny candy. There
was still *two*-for-a-penny candy.

So I still bend.
Inflation has not touched the child
in my psyche. Even when my brain
knows otherwise, that child delights at *gift*,

as if the day itself had bent
and blessed me.

Heirlooms

I have given away the silver brooch
that found its way to me out of my one
grandmother's possessions after she died.
I have given away the gold ring my other
grandmother gave me when I was 13.
I have given them to my oldest niece's
daughter. For years I kept the ring and the
brooch in a box, looked at them sometimes
with puzzlement: *what could they be to me?*

I have never wondered that about the prayer book
my father gave me when he was dying.
It had been his grandmother's. It is battered,
water-stained. I cannot read it. It is in two
languages that are not mine. I recognize
some of the Latin words, phrases, whole
prayers: *Pater, Credo, Ave.*

Its other language is Breton, which descended
only to my grandparents. From placement,
from parallels with the Latin, I recognize the word
for *God*. From similarity to Latin or French,
the words for *power, will, truth*. But I cannot
read it.

Sometimes I leaf through it, try to make meaning
of the words. I think, *My great-grandmother
prayed with this. My father read perhaps the Latin,
      made out perhaps more of the Breton than I do.*
When he knew he was dying, he chose me
among his children to have it.

It lives on a shelf among my other books.
When I pick it up and browse through it,
I am with my father, with his grandmother
praying.

Crone

The skin on my back will thicken.
Little brown armies of bumps
will climb up my neck to where
already there is a permanent tan.
My skin will be spots and flakes
and bumps and slackness.

A caress will encounter
multitudinous small obstacles
but will be a caress all the same.
Thick tough hairs will sprout
in unexpected places (thigh,
belly, nipple) and more expected
ones (lip, chin, nostril).

My bones will turn brittle and
porous. But if my spine bends,
my spirit straightens as I become
lighter. My head will be in the wind,
drunk with wind.

I will be wrinkled and my flesh will
sag in folds that sing siren songs
to the earth. But my eyes will be
clear as I enter the time of my power.
I grow strong, I grow deep
as the mask thickens.

All my ghosts are useful

I am multiply haunted and
all my ghosts are useful.

They are the webbing on the parachute,
the rope in the hammock, the frame
of the house. They are my depth and
dimension. They determine
the boundaries of my
self. Without them, I would
not be real.

They make the track in the trackless desert.
They are the feet of God in my night.
They are angels guiding me.
They are the marching invisible army
around me through dark forests.
They are everything that makes me
not solitary.

Nothing that haunts me is useless.
My ghosts call me out of sleep and they
call me back to it. They know all my names.

Still in the world

What's in this box? I think,
reaching up to the highest shelf
for the blue box that once held writing paper.

I leaf through a collection of notes from
past students, faded letters from
long-lost friends, and there

is the *In memoriam* card
your father handed out to all the staff
after the funeral.

Here you are, your photo, your name,
your age at time of death (18 years
and 5 months).

You had a summer job washing windows.
You were on a scaffold anchored
to the roof of the hospital
                              when
the anchor on one side gave way and tipped you
off the end. The harness held, but the fall
swung you against the wall and cracked your skull.

I worked for your father. After the funeral,
he came back to work brittle
and brave and tearless, as is required of men.
He gave us each a card with your photo.

Here you are, smiling in the sun
over 30 years later, still in the world
in some form. And that, perhaps,

is what your father wanted.

With new eyes

I slept for several years, a spell upon me
of stagnation, of death.
I had mouldering dreams in which
I turned into most of the human shapes
which in my youth
I rejected.

I lost the sky,
hungered for simple plots,
sought comfort in mere things.

I thought I was waiting for an end to time,
but I was waiting for a waking.

It came slowly, beginning as joy, as wonder.
I opened eyes that had never been mine before,
eyes that loved a leaf, a cloud, a blade of new grass,
as if each was the first of its kind in the world.

Then peace came—the sensual slow awakening
to what the body could give—the comfort of
a warm bed, a long close hug.

Then, here and there, pain came too,
sudden twinges or deep aches.
Fear gathered in the shadows under hedges.

Tears and turbulence are new again,
as wonder came back new.

Here on the far side of a long dead sleep,
I am awake
with new eyes.

Letter looking forward

I want this letter to tell the truth—about me,
about the morning, about where I am in
literal and less literal ways.

I want to send you the sheer blue of this
crisp morning after the season's first frost,
the gold and green of elm leaves and the darker green
of conifers, the sharp fine black of twigs and branches.
I want to catch the glint of sun off passing traffic,
the smell of coffee, the clatter of dishes, and the hum
of other people's conversation in this coffee shop
where I have come alone to be with you by letter.
I want you to inhabit this space which my words on paper
inhabit as they incline towards you.

If I can find the words for here and now, perhaps
I can find the words for you and me.

This morning I was merciless in my housekeeping,
consigned pounds of paper to recycling. That too
is a push at truth.

I want this letter to be as true as the colours
of the first morning after frost, as clean
as the rinsed blue sky. I have clung too long
to silence, have let my thoughts drift formless
until I am formless too.

Before I send you my words, I want them
as sharp and spare as I can make them.

>I am not sure what I hope from you.
>I fear traps.
>I have illusions and
>a hunger so deep
>I am afraid to let it speak.
>
>You are the only man I
>have ever met
>who does not make me
>think of traps.
>
>I thought I had stopped wanting,
>but I want you.

As I write this, we are days since our last meeting,
months before we meet again. We have a shared history
of which your memory and mine are not quite the same.
We have each a past in which are huge pieces
we will never share except as they have made us
who we are.

This is the morning after the first frost in a city
of clear skies half a country from where you live.
I have a winter's time to clear away the clutter,
to pull up my life from where it cannot root,
and move in your direction, following
these words.

Even love

Even love can find me
who thought I would never be found,

who thought I was invisible
to anything big enough to be called
passion,

who thought I would only know
distance and who welcomed
even pain and loss because they told me
I was alive.

I thought I was too small
to be seen.
I thought I was too far away
to be found.

Even love can find me.
Love can find even me.

The real world

Ice fog

A rainbow shattered in the cold
and its shards hang
suspended over the city.

The air shimmers with hints
of every colour in the spectrum.
Ghost colours, pearly and faint,
now here, now gone,
as ice crystals drift in the muted light.

The city is transformed into its best self,
essence of winter,
clean,

so beautiful that it doesn't matter
that each tiny crystal
is sharp as a needle
to the nostrils, to the lungs,
that every breath cuts.

I bundle in layers, wrap a scarf
across my face to filter
the million tiny needles,
and go for a walk.

Not many people are out.
Not many people want to be.

But I cannot resist this chance
to walk through the heart
of rainbow, to see it
glinting faint on every side,

to inhale
its broken fire.

Every morning

Every morning a boy waters the sidewalk
in front of McDonalds. He uses a black hose
attached to the faucet in the red brick wall.
Sometimes he waters the red brick wall too,
washing dust from the graffiti so that
they stand out boldly, black scrawl on red
brick: a happy face, an obscenity, *No air*.
He waters the dust, the concrete, the absence
of any green growing thing.

The slow hush of water competes with
traffic noise: small gurglings, tiny streams,
placid flat surfaces where the sidewalk
traps small lakes. He waters the whole sidewalk,
wall to curb, careless of the feet of passersby
who step gingerly through his small flood,
careless too of the black snake of the hose
uncoiling behind him, nipping at people's feet
with sudden loops.

The boy waters the sidewalk as if it were
a lawn or a garden. He waters the wall.
The graffiti flower. The concrete whispers
gratefully, like leaves in rain.

In the ravines

In the ravines that cut the city
at ragged intervals, I go walking with a friend.

In the ravines in the spring,
chickadees eat from your hand.
Tiny claws tickle your palm
as they land to grab a seed.
They follow you down the trail
in small clouds of shadow-
coloured quick movement.

In the ravines all year round,
wild boar live. They have escaped
from game farms and found refuge
in the wilderness at the heart of the city.
They are shy of the joggers, cyclists,
walkers, and dogs who use the trails.

Nobody ever sees them, but they are there,
as surely as the chickadees.
They are the darkest shadows indistinct
among the bushes when night falls.

Men in hard hats

They have closed off the bridge
so that men in hard hats and fluorescent vests
can converse uninterrupted with the girders.
They stand, each with a clipboard,
confronting aged steel, noting the inroads
of rust, diagnosing. They mark their decisions
indelibly on steel. They write for themselves
notes at greater length on paper.

They commune with the effects of passing
time on steel and stone, with the elements,
with the slow wearing out of all things exposed
to sun and wind and temperature.

The men wear fluorescence, as if in danger
of being lost among the girders and beams.
They wear protective hats and boots, as if even
before they touch the bridge with anything more
powerful than their markers, the bridge could
damage them.

                    As if it could sense
their surgical intentions: those drills and hammers.
As if it could, if it so wished, drop them
in the river or crush them under stone.

They face the girders with respect, their faces
serious.

The man who plays musical instruments

All of them, it seems. He is three-quarters
of a band: keyboard, guitar, percussion,
and the voice in the background that blends
sweetly with the lead. He is not in the limelight
but take him away and all you have left
is a guitar and a voice alone. He is
the texture.

He picks up any instrument and plays it.
He orders a Celtic harp, specially made, and masters it
in a couple of weeks. In his apartment, the guest room
is also the music room where live the harp, the guitar,
the synthesizer, the drum machine, a banjo and
probably several other instruments.

He is the man with music, though he tries
other things, lives other lives.
He is photographer. He is writer. He is
connoisseur of art. He is doctor. "I have to go
save lives," he says, and goes to work.

But he is the man with music.

This scientist

This scientist specializes in minute microbial
life from the swamps of northern Canada,
forms of life that had no name (to us—to them
they were them) until she caught them in her
clean glass containers and held them under
microscopes, probed and defined them.
Several small life forms bear her name.
It is like naming stars—a kind of
immortality.

I imagine her in hip waders in smelly places
other people avoid, bending over reeds and
swamp water, reading the scum, the textures
of live water, the glyphs of stirred up mud.
In my mind, it is always a cloudy day and the land
flat with no sign anywhere of human life
except the scientist and her tools. In my mind,
she is here most fully herself, most content.

The real world

In her presence I am automatically
apologetic, too different from her to find
a common ground or to feel like a fellow
citizen in the real world.

She is of course the one who lives
in the real world. She is a scientist and
administrator. She deals in stats and
schedules and contracts, things clearcut
and measurable.

I am a poet. I work in the realm of no
final answers. I haunt a borderland
whose further edges fade into mist
so that the hills behind me vanish in a blur:
no clear lines, no definition.

Even when she tells me she admires
what I do that she cannot, she stands on solid
ground, and I waver like a mirage before
the blunt straightforward solidity
of her voice and self.

Where the railyards were (Edmonton 1998)

The college takes up three blocks, its turrets
knifing the sky. A casino pushes its new concrete
parking lot against the wilderness of weeds that stretches
back to the wornout warehouses that used to be
on the wrong side of the tracks. The raw new frames
of condos rise out of the mud, daily changing
their shape against the sky.

The city is reclaiming the abandoned yards where
the tracks used to snake and weave and now are gone.
But there are still vast spaces of ragged weed-strewn
grass that in the summer grows rough among the hummocks
where the railyards were. Blanks in the middle of the city,
where sky and wind are unobstructed and where signs
at intervals warn of unspecified *Hidden dangers.*

Hidden dangers in the junk dropped by those
taking shortcuts: bottles whole or broken, odd bits
of railyard junk, pieces of metal that once were pieces
of something useful. Hidden dangers in the predatory life
lurking patient in the long grass: animal life or insect life or
human life. Rabbit holes to fall into, fairy rings to spirit
you away, invisible spaceships to harvest you
as specimen.

In broad daylight taking a shortcut across an innocent
empty space, you disappear. Perhaps forever. Perhaps
for 10 minutes or 10 seconds, and nobody notices,
not even you.

All you notice is that you come out the other side
bewildered, nagged by a half-memory you will
never pin down.
                As if you have entered one facet of a prism
and come out a neighbouring one—everything shifted
so slightly that you are not quite sure (though you could
almost swear) that even what still looks the same

is not.

Cat Among the Boots

Cat Among the Boots, she thinks,
looking up to see the cat posed among
the boots in the hall closet.

She gives names to the sudden pictures
her eye frames and freezes.

Wednesday Morning, 6:30 a.m.:
winter; the sun not up; snowlight
and shadows in the alley.

Rain on the Window:
slow drops glinting between
two lights—outside, the streetlight
on a deserted street; inside,
the light in her rooms.

She does this only in solitude,
only with moments free of other people,
though in art it is faces she loves, not
landscapes, not still life.

She does not want to paint,
only to name the still moments
and by naming, hold them.

Northern morning meditation

I ride the half-empty bus to work
in the pre-dawn winter darkness.
Houses are frail shells under the weight
of night, brave islands in the sea
of blackness. I wrap my solitude
around me, riding west when
the rush is eastward.

The bus leaves me on a sleeping
sidestreet and takes its noise away
into the crisp not-yet-day. Sky
looms over me, vast and hollow.
I am alone in air that feels as pure
as the first breath in the world.

Earth is a flatness emphasizing sky.
Every break in the flatness is merely
a dent: the high banks of snow around
the parking lot, the low building
in which I work, even the black bulk
of Superstore across the street.

The sky pulls at my eyes as I walk
briefly east, where the black shades into
violet. As the days push towards spring,
violet yields to deep blue yields to
pink and gold. But it is this in-between
that pulls at me, this deep violet, almost
black, barely hinting at day.

In this pause between the noise of
the bus and the noise of the working day,
I am part of the arching sky: its high space,
its deep intaken breath.

Slow morning at the coffeeshop

One server reads a tabloid headline
aloud to the other: *Woman gives birth
to monkey.* They speculate about
the state of mind of this mother,
joke about her sex life, tell their
weird dreams.

One customer reads a newspaper.
Two converse in low voices.
The radio plays in the background.

January in Edmonton. The world
outside the windows has forgotten colour:
grey-white clouds hang in a low sky;
trees shake their black twigs against the clouds;
grey wind sucks moisture from the snow
along the sidewalks; the street is so dry
it might crumble at a touch.

Traffic is light, exhaust fumes ragged.
Even on Jasper Avenue, even on
Saturday morning, only the occasional
pedestrian, hands in pockets, hood
pulled high.

Icicles

The view from my living room window
is jagged with icicles.
They break the straight line of the eaves
with their asymmetry. They create a foreground
to the background of highrises and thin
winter trees. They complicate
what had been a simple picture in a simple
frame.

The biggest icicle grows down
from the corner where the annex I live in
connects with the main building.
I cannot see its roots on the roof, can only imagine
the rivulets of ice that contribute to its bulk.
But the part I *can* see, the part I could touch
if I opened the window,
is as big as I am.

I have never been so close
to an icicle this big.
It bulges like the muscles of a bodybuilder.
It gleams with muted greys, greens, browns.
I walk under its silent menace every day.

At the first hint of thaw, the caretaker
climbs onto the roof with an axe. I hear
his footsteps over my head, then the blows
of the axe. He is up there a long time,
his blows concentrated on the corner where
the annex joins the main building.

When he leaves, the view has become
a broken-toothed grin, like the aftermath
of a brawl.

Only the biggest icicle remains
unscarred, its menace
intact.

A skunk that dies on Saskatchewan Drive

A skunk that dies on Saskatchewan Drive
sends the news of its death
wafting through the summer night
into the open windows of the highrises,
tickles the nostrils of sleepers
with messages as potent as the sudden
voice of the morning radio.

In the highrises along the edge of the valley,
with the downtown skyline winking
across the distance, people
wrinkle their nostrils in their sleep
but cannot stay there. They wake
into the cloud of the skunk's death.
They cough, pull pillows over their faces,
or get up and close the window
against the violence.

A skunk that crosses Saskatchewan Drive
at the wrong moment of a quiet summer night
sends death pushing into the dreams of
sleepers, turns the night
unquiet.

Millennial weather

The food court provides shelter
from the rain—a sudden downpour
once again. Every day this week,
the sky dumps. Every next day,
the sun pokes through the haze,
sucks the water back into the clouds,
turns the air thick, the sky to haze.

On the dry prairies, this is
millennial weather, out of character and
uneasy. It makes us itch in the skin
of the soul, as if one day the downpour
will settle in for good, another Flood.

The food court is crowded. Children
shriek. Conversation mutters and
shuffles, a closer thunder than the one
outside. Three floors up, the domed
glass roof is so slick with rain it could be
melting.

Lights flicker. I plan my exit, in case
the power fails: *stay put until the rush
and panic are past; trust the distant
sky, what light it gives.*

Late October, late afternoon in the office

In slow motion, the fax machine ingests one sheet of
the 20 I am sending. It pauses, savours, spits it out,
ingests another, pauses.

It is afternoon coffee break. I face a long open
space of desks, each with computer, where a dozen
people normally work but which now is still.

The year's first snowfall dims the daylight,
blurs the distance outside the windows. In the stillness,
faintly from a radio somewhere, I hear *Flashdance*.

In late afternoon snowlight, while my co-workers are
somewhere else talking and drinking coffee, while the fax
machine pauses, ingests, pauses, spits, in its wondrous
non-human rhythm, and my workless fingers wait, my feet
catch the rhythm of the distant radio, and
                              I dance.

At the next table

Politicians at the next table in the coffeeshop.
Not major politicians. Nobody you would ever see
in a newspaper photo, except maybe dimly behind
somebody's elbow. These are the hopeful
future, loud and braggart. Groupies perhaps.
Volunteers. Maybe even paid help eager to taste
power.

I was wrong to choose this table over the one
near the child of shrieking age.

The politicians drop names loudly, pass
judgment and hotel room gossip. They argue
allegiance and change of allegiance.

                        (To be fair,
they are not all loud. Some speak barely above
a whisper, as if hinting to the others, who do not
catch hints.)

                      They argue image and instinct,
charisma and its absence. They know that everyone
in the coffeeshop is blessed by proximity to their
proximity to power.

An infant screams from a far corner of the room.
I would like to be on the far side of that scream.

Coffee break

The woman with the carrying voice is at
a table for two with a quiet companion. She
dominates every conversation in the cafeteria. She
dominates the kitchen clatter. She dominates
my attempts to focus my thoughts at my table alone.

Against my will, I hear that she has been passed over
for promotion; that her new home is costing
a sacrilegious amount in unexpected repairs; that
her husband is the parent of preference because
he is not strict about bedtime. She presents these
laments in mellow reasonable tones from which
poke small thorns.

She must want to please her table companion,
whose part in the conversation reaches me only
as a murmur—as if she were talking to herself,
with occasional pauses. Talks, talks, talks.

                      Eventually,
the thorns in her voice settle down. He must have
a soothing effect on her. From this distance, he is bland,
his voice an undercurrent, thick and dark to hers.

The thorns in her bright carrying voice
settle into that undercurrent, pull in their heads—
like a cat pulling in its claws, smoothing its fur, tucking
its paws against its body, considering
                                    sleep.

But

She is not pretty

but

I like her face
because she looks a lot
like somebody I
don't like

but

she is not pretty

A ritual goodbye

His naked limbs were so slick with oil
and he so limp with drunkenness
they could barely hold onto him
when they pulled him out of
the stag party practical joke.
They had stripped him and hung him
by his bound hands
in a barrel of oil, and they had
poured alcohol down his helpless throat.

The muscles of his back and shoulders
gleamed smooth and beautiful with youth
and strength. His chest, his thighs,
his legs looked as if molded from
some new kind of stone that shone
with its own light—like a Michelangelo
sculpture gone limp.

This was his farewell from the world
of the man's man, his hazing into
servitude to a woman. The oil would not
wash from his skin, so they turned
a heavy hose on him, blasting him free
the way you blast brick clean
with sand.

The man who told the story still laughed about it
years later. I thought of the bridegroom
waking to the worst hangover of his life
and every muscle sore from the pounding water.

I thought of his bride receiving his punished
flesh into her own, embracing the body battered
inside and out by the ritual goodbye
of his friends.

Neighbour

She asks if I work at a local bar.
She can't account for my irregular
comings and goings. Later, she asks
if I'm a nun. Perhaps she has peered
through my windows and seen the stark
black and white Crucifixion
on my wall.

She lives next door and spends hours
on yard work. When she runs out of yard,
she rakes the boulevard. If she ran out
of boulevard, she would carry over
into the park across the street.

She is always outside. I can't come
or go without running the gauntlet of her
questions. She doesn't hide her curiosity,
or even try to disguise it. She is insatiable.
I volunteer nothing, and I ask no questions.
I answer hers, but without elaboration.
What she doesn't know, she invents,
and no doubt spreads to the neighbours.

In this neighbourhood where I am
a stranger, I have a shifting identity.
I am a nun who works at a bar, serving
drinks and bantering with customers,
or blessing them. I drop prayers
among the jokes and curses. I finger
like a rosary the coins that pass
through my fingers,
each coin a prayer.

Upon my skin

Heat presses against my skin, emphatic,
demanding, wherever I am uncovered.
Sun heat fuses with body heat, pulling
to the surface the darkening that on me
is deep gold. If I were blonde, I would
be a summer goddess.

I am not blonde, and what it does is
draw in deeper blue the lines of veins,
dramatize the fragility of wrist bone,
so that skeleton becomes visible. The
heat presses down, curdles the even tones
of the skin. It pulls slackness into wrinkles,
strokes the dormant cancer cells,
coaxing.

I am a sacrifice to the sun, offered up
to celebrate its powers of transformation.
Upon my skin, it scrawls its patient
signature.

End of the day in the student coffeehouse

Coffee from the last pot of the day is ominously dark,
as if it contained the bitterest dregs of all the previous pots—
remnants of one poured into the next until the day's heaviest
history is distilled here: jealousy, vindictiveness, anxiety, fear.

Here is the venom of the discarded lover watching a successor;
the shrunken loneliness of unrequited love; the quarrels of
old friends or new lovers; exam anxiety and the fear
of never being anyone but who you are
this very moment—vague, without direction,
surrounded by shining success that never looks your way.

Everything satisfying and sustaining has been poured out
steaming and aromatic: new love, the promise of tomorrow,
long deep conversations that stir the soul and change the self.

Coffee from the last pot of the day will do its job: it will give you
the jolt that can keep you working another hour or two, keep you
awake through the long evening class. But it has sat too long
to retain the buoyant full taste of the morning's first.
It is a thick bitter silt, business only.

From my office window

I thought she was kicking at the leaves
as she walks across the soccer field
leaning hard against the wind,
but she has a bouncy little brown thing
on a leash and seems to be kicking
some object for it to chase.
I can't see the object. It's too far and
I forgot my glasses again.
I can't even see for sure
if the bouncy brown thing is a dog,
though it must be. Cats don't come
in that shade of brown and don't
walk so willingly on leashes.
It could of course be some entirely
different bouncy animal, and *she*
might even be *he* in these days
of indiscriminately cultivated long hair.
It's just that I think I recognize
that blob of blue as a particular sweater
that goes with that colour of yellow hair
on a particular person.
I should have remembered my glasses.
Then I could have spoken with certainty
about the dog and the nature of the
object kicked and whether the walker
is *she* or *he* and maybe even told you
who. She is gone now and the dog too,
or whatever it was, and the soccer field
is empty of detail, though if I had my glasses
it might not be.

PD Day in the historic train station

Where the railway tracks used to run
are bicycle paths and lawn. The train station
retains nothing of its former purpose: meetings,
partings, arrival, departure, movement, change.
It is a conference centre now, and the meetings
that happen here are more mundane.

On this spring day, civil servants are gathered
under duress for carefully orchestrated fun
according to some professional idea of what that means.
They call that somebody a *facilitator*, a *motivational
speaker*. They call the process *professional development*.

We play games that mimic friendship with people
who are (or not) friends in very specific
daily-contact ways where intimacy has clear boundaries.
We pretend to cross those boundaries, but we are
careful: we have too many tomorrows
still to spend together.

High above us, in the halfmoon windows, under
the vaulted ceiling, echoes of all kinds sleep:
greetings and goodbyes, loudspeaker announcements,
distantly the trains. Echoes of the city's past,
the city's change and movement.

Spring sun touches the stone walls, moving
slowly as the hours move, never reaching
low enough to touch us.

The speaker speaks. We go through the motions,
motivated towards the *Exit* sign, the spring
daylight, the outdoor air.

Renovation

Somebody is living in the house that was
closed for months after a fire, its roof
heavy with fangs of ice, its windows boarded up,
frozen black flame radiating from the blank
new wood where the door had been.

Now the boards are gone from the windows.
Smoke rises only from the chimney.
Electric light glows quietly.

For a while, through uncurtained windows,
you could see the scars of its trauma: doorways gnawed
black, paint in blisters. In every room, the smell
of fire death still clung stronger than those of
sawdust and new plaster.

Behind the house, a dumpster collects debris.
In a room at the front, a television screen glows blue.

The house is resurrecting: dead flesh methodically
cut away, scar tissue mended, new bone transplanted.
Curtains replace the open stare that replaced the plywood.
The walls around the scarred doorway acquire
new wood, then the mesh to hold stucco.

No one would guess the ghost of fire terror
beneath new wood and plaster. Another day, another
week, and it is not a resurrection but just another
renovation.

Pushing the wind

The sky is grey haze.
The grass lies low,
leaning north.

I lean south,
pushing the wind.

A whirlwind dances
in the gravel parking lot,
tossing a grey cloud
into my face.

I lean into the wind
as into arms.

The sun is doused in grey
but my mind
glitters and sparkles
like stone in sunlight,
dances
like dust in wind.

Old winter

The snow is tired. It has thawed
and frozen, thawed and frozen, and its edges
have become ice crystal, blank space, and dirt.

When it was fresh, it caught and held
every speck of dust, froze every wandering
bit of trash. Now it releases
one by one a winter's
worth.

The snow is broken, worn, faded grey,
pocked with dirt where the sun
has probed.

Even the new soft white
fresh from last night
cannot cover the scars, cannot disguise
how old this winter is.

Some of these poems have appeared, sometimes in earlier versions, in *Amethyst Review, Arc, Contemporary Verse 2, Dandelion, Event, North American Review, Prairie Journal, Prairie Fire, Queen's Quarterly, Room of One's Own, Spire Poetry Poster, The Antigonish Review, The New Quarterly* and in the anthologies *Stroll of Poets: The 1998 Anthology, Literature & Media II, Passages: Literature and Language, Threshold: An Anthology of Contemporary Writing in Alberta*, and *Decalogue: Ten Ottawa Poets*. Others have appeared online at www.bywords.ca and www.ottawater.com.

Anne Le Dressay grew up in Manitoba, first on a farm near Virden and then on an acreage outside Lorette. She has lived for extended periods in Winnipeg, Ottawa, and Edmonton (in that order). She taught English and Creative Writing for ten years in Alberta. She is now in Ottawa for the second time, working for the feds. She has been publishing sporadically since the 1970's. She has one book, *Sleep Is a Country* (Harbinger, 1997) and two chapbooks, *This Body That I Live In* (Turnstone, 1979) and *Woman Dreams* (above/ground, 1998).

Acknowledgements:

I would like to thank my family and friends for ongoing support and encouragement, especially the following: David Anderson, Vish Chawla, Ray Corrin, Rusti Lehay, Dan Le Dressay, Monique Le Dressay, Tom Lips, Diana McCarthy, Lynne McCarthy, Naomi McIlwraith, Hans Posthuma, Linda Posthuma, Robert Stanley, Linnéa Rowlatt, Ruth Vanderwoude, Carrie Villeneuve. Very particular thanks to rob mclennan for editorial help on this manuscript, to Jennifer Mulligan for painstaking care to the design and technical detail of the finished product, and to Heather Spears for permission to use her sketch on the back cover.

Other titles from Chaudiere Books:

A Long Continual Argument: The Selected Poems of John Newlove. John Newlove, poetry.
   Robert McTavish, editor. 978-0-9781601-9-7
Collected Sex. Poetry anthology, rob mclennan, editor. 978-0-9781601-8-0
Decalogue: ten Ottawa poets. rob mclennan, editor. 978-0-9781601-3-5
Decalogue2: ten Ottawa fiction writers. rob mclennan, editor. 978-0-9781601-4-2
Disappointment Island. Monty Reid, poetry. 978-0-9781601-1-1
Everything is Movies. Nicholas Lea, poetry. 978-0-9781601-7-3
Movements in Jars. Meghan Jackson, poetry. 978-0-9781601-0-4
The Desmond Road Book of the Dead. Clare Latremouille, fiction. 978-0-9781601-2-8
The Ottawa City Project. rob mclennan, poetry. 978-0-9781601-6-6
There Is No Mountain: Selected Poems of Andrew Suknaski. Andrew Suknaski, poetry.
   rob mclennan, editor. 978-0-9781601-5-9